J

D0757795

World's WEIRDEST Animals

Proboscis Monkeys

Big Buddy Books

An Imprint of Abdo Publishing
abdopublishing.com

Marcia Zappa

abdopublishing.com

Published by Abdo Publishing, a division of ABDO, PO Box 398166, Minneapolis, Minnesota 55439. Copyright © 2016 by Abdo Consulting Group, Inc. International copyrights reserved in all countries. No part of this book may be reproduced in any form without written permission from the publisher. Big Buddy Books™ is a trademark and logo of Abdo Publishing.

Printed in the United States of America, North Mankato, Minnesota.
042015
092015

Cover Photos: Shutterstock.com.
Interior Photos: ©iStockphoto.com (pp. 11, 17); jspix/Glow Images (pp. 9, 27); Thomas Marent/Minden Pictures
      (p. 21); Louise Murray/Glow Images (pp. 7, 15); Adam Seward/Glow Images (p. 5); Anup Shah/NPL/
      Minden Pictures (pp. 19, 25); Shutterstock.com (pp. 23, 29, 30).

Coordinating Series Editor: Rochelle Baltzer
Contributing Editors: Megan M. Gunderson, Bridget O'Brien, Sarah Tieck
Graphic Design: Adam Craven

Library of Congress Cataloging-in-Publication Data

Zappa, Marcia, 1985- author.
  Proboscis monkeys / Marcia Zappa.
      pages cm. -- (World's weirdest animals)
  ISBN 978-1-62403-777-1
1. Proboscis monkey--Juvenile literature. I. Title.
  QL737.P93Z37 2016
  599.8'6--dc23
                        2015005569

Contents

Wildly Weird!

The world is full of weird, wonderful animals. Proboscis (pruh-BAH-suhs) monkeys are known for their long noses. In fact, *proboscis* means "long nose."

These monkeys live in forests near water in Southeast Asia. They have unusually strong swimming skills. These features make proboscis monkeys wildly weird!

Did You Know?

Only adult male proboscis monkeys have famously large noses. An adult female's nose looks like a male's, but it is much smaller. A young proboscis monkey has an upturned nose.

Proboscis monkeys live in trees. They sometimes search for food on the ground. But, this is uncommon.

Super Sniffer

An adult male proboscis monkey's nose can be more than four inches (10 cm) long! Scientists believe a male's large nose helps it get a **mate**. They think it helps make a male's call loud. This **impresses** females. And, it scares off other males.

If a male proboscis monkey gets upset, its nose may swell and turn red.

7

Bold Bodies

Proboscis monkeys are **mammals**. Their bodies are covered in fur.

An adult's fur is reddish brown on its head, shoulders, back, and thighs. It is light gray on its tail and its lower arms and legs. Tan or light orange skin covers the monkey's face.

Most adult proboscis monkeys have a collar of cream fur around their necks.

Proboscis monkeys have big, round bellies. They have long, thin arms and legs. And, they have long tails.

Proboscis monkeys are large. They grow to be 21 to 30 inches (53 to 76 cm) long. Adults weigh 15 to 48 pounds (7 to 22 kg). Males are much larger than females.

Did You Know?
A proboscis monkey's tail is about as long as its body.

NOSE

TAIL

ARM

LEG

BELLY

Where in the World?

Proboscis monkeys live on the island of Borneo in Southeast Asia. Borneo belongs to three countries. These are Brunei, Malaysia, and Indonesia.

Proboscis monkeys are found near water. Often, they live in swampy **mangrove** forests near the coast. Some live farther inland in forests near rivers.

Did You Know?

Proboscis monkeys are rarely found more than 0.6 miles (1 km) from water.

Europe

Asia

Africa

N
W ✦ E
S

Pacific Ocean

Brunei
Malaysia
BORNEO
Indonesia

■ = Proboscis Monkey Region

Australia

A Monkey's Life

Most proboscis monkeys live in groups called harems. These groups have about 20 monkeys. They include one adult male, up to 12 adult females, and their young. Males without a harem live together in **bachelor** groups.

The adult male is the leader of the harem. He decides where the group goes.

Proboscis monkeys use both arms and both legs to move easily through treetops. During the day, they rest, eat, move around, and **groom** each other.

Proboscis monkeys make sounds and movements to share their thoughts and feelings. Adult males growl to calm other members of their harems. They honk to scare off **predators**. Females and young monkeys scream loudly when they are angry or excited.

Did You Know?

Proboscis monkeys have few predators in their treetop homes. Clouded leopards hunt them on the ground. And, crocodiles hunt them in the water.

Groups of proboscis monkeys come together at night. They sleep in one or more trees near water.

Strong Swimmers

Proboscis monkeys must move around to find food. Sometimes, they have to cross rivers. These monkeys have an unusual skill. They are excellent swimmers! They have partially **webbed** hands and feet. They can swim up to 65 feet (20 m) underwater.

Did You Know?

Proboscis monkeys are such fast swimmers they can escape crocodiles!

Proboscis monkeys are known to leap out of trees into the water. They often do belly flops!

Favorite Foods

Proboscis monkeys mainly eat young leaves. They often eat the leaves of the **mangrove** trees they live in. They also eat seeds, fruit, flowers, and some bugs. In all, these monkeys eat more than 90 different types of plants!

An adult male proboscis monkey's nose often hangs in front of his mouth. He may need to move it out of the way to eat.

Proboscis monkeys use their thumbs to tear off plant parts. Their sharp back teeth rip apart their food. And, their stomachs are specially built to **digest** it.

Did You Know?

Proboscis monkeys only eat fruit that is not yet ripe. Ripe fruit can get stuck in the stomach, causing it to fill with gas. This can lead to death.

It takes a long time for a proboscis monkey to digest its food. So, it is usually full. That is why its belly is so big and round.

Life Cycle

The females in a harem **compete** to **mate** with the group's male. After five to six months, a mother proboscis monkey gives birth to one baby. It has a blue face and dark fur.

24

As a baby grows, its skin and fur change color.

Mothers work hard to care for their babies. They carry them and clean them. And, they provide milk for them to drink.

Babies stay with their mothers for about one year. Then, females become members of the harem. Males leave to join a **bachelor** group.

A baby drinks its mother's milk for about seven months.

World Wide Weird

Proboscis monkeys were once common. Sadly, they have lost much of their **habitat**. People cut down trees for lumber and used land for buildings and farms. Today, these monkeys are **endangered**.

It is important to know how our actions affect wild animals. Through change, we may be able to keep weird, wonderful animals such as proboscis monkeys around for years to come.

People work to keep proboscis monkeys safe. Parts of their habitat are protected. And, there are laws against hunting and capturing them.

FAST FACTS ABOUT:
Proboscis Monkeys

Animal Type – mammal

Size – 21 to 30 inches (53 to 76 cm) long

Weight – 15 to 48 pounds (7 to 22 kg)

Habitat – forests near water on the island of Borneo

Diet – young leaves, seeds, fruit, flowers, and bugs

What makes the proboscis monkey wildly weird?

Adult males have noses that can be more than four inches (10 cm) long! And, proboscis monkeys are known for their super swimming skills.

Glossary

bachelor a male without a mate.

compete to take part in a contest between two or more animals, persons, or groups.

digest (deye-JEHST) to break down food into parts small enough for the body to use.

endangered in danger of dying out.

groom to clean and care for.

habitat a place where a living thing is naturally found.

impress to gain the admiration or interest of.

mammal a member of a group of living beings. Mammals make milk to feed their babies and usually have hair or fur on their skin.

mangrove a tree with roots that grow from its branches. It grows in swamps or shallow salt water.

mate to join as a couple in order to reproduce, or have babies. A mate is a partner to join with in order to reproduce.

predator a person or animal that hunts and kills animals for food.

webbed having fingers or toes that are joined together with skin, or webs.

Websites

To learn more about World's Weirdest Animals, visit **booklinks.abdopublishing.com**. These links are routinely monitored and updated to provide the most current information available.

Index